Explosion of Hope

POETRY & PROSE FOR THE SOUL

by

Carolyn Kristos French

Ark House Press
arkhousepress.com

Cataloguing in Publication Data:
Title: Explosion of Hope
ISBN: 978-1-7638801-9-1 (pbk)
Subjects: REL012040 RELIGION / Christian Living / Inspirational; REL077000 RELIGION / Faith; POE003000 POETRY / Subjects & Themes / Religious.

Design by initiateagency.com

Contents

Preamble

All of us have ups and downs in life. Some have harder lives than others. This book is Part 1 of my attempt to paint a word picture of my faith in Christ whilst dealing with the fallout from my first marriage. In essence I married the wrong person and ended up in a domestic violence situation, living with a paedophile, who has since suicided.

My second marriage was to a man I called my 'Mr. Wonderful'. He was so totally the opposite to my first husband in every way. My 'Mr. Wonderful' has now gone home to be with Jesus where he is free from cancer.

Along life's journey, I have also encountered others living with various types of mental or emotional pain and grief. We all handle pain differently. I chose to choose faith in Jesus Christ to get me through life's darkest hours.

Jesus Christ is my mainstay, my rock, my hope, and my hope has increased as the years have passed. There is hope and light, be it ever so dim in the darkest of places in life. Hope gets brighter until it explodes inside of us as we keep our focus on Jesus Christ.

Has the journey been easy? Definitely not!
But has hope made it worthwhile? Yes, Yes and Yes!

Carolyn Kristos French

For *it is* the God who commanded light to shine out of darkness, who has shone in our hearts to give the light of the knowledge of the glory of God in the face of Jesus Christ. But we have this treasure in earthen vessels, that the excellence of the power may be of God and not of us.

2 Corinthians 4:6-7 NKJV

My Soul Cries Out

ME: My soul cries out, "Blessed be Your Name".

GOD: I love you, my child, my daughter, my beautiful one. I have loved you with an everlasting love and I will not deny it.

ME: My soul cries out, "Blessed be Your Name".

GOD: Come away my bride, my lover, come away and feast on Me and with Me. I long for your presence, your company, your love, your desire. Come away and be Mine.

ME: My soul cries out, "Blessed be Your Name".

You, O Lord, are the desire of all nations. You are my heart's desire. With my whole being I desire You, to know You in a way which will satisfy and purify my longings for You.

My soul cries out "Blessed be Your Name".

***

Wedding Prayer

Lord, I am preparing for my wedding
As You alone do know.
I pray my Lord, my soul to keep
As You join me to this man.

I pray that our two hearts,
Will be melded into one.
That this one heart would beat
According to Your drum.

I pray my Lord, this man
Would love me as You do.
I pray my love for him
Would love him through and through.

I pray our love for You
Will grow deeper day by day.
I pray my Lord, our souls to keep
On this our wedding day.

***

Refreshing in Psalm 23

The Lord is my right hand man.
He gives me peace and quiet.
He refreshes my emotions.
He leads me in paths of righteousness
For His Name's sake.

Even though I am overwhelmed
And it looks dark around me,
I see the light beckoning me onward,
Calling me forth,
And through the misty way
Into brilliant sunshine.

I will fear no evil for You are here with me,
Taking me by the hand.
You do not allow me to walk alone,
For You know the way that I must take,
And even though the path seems treacherous,
Your light is leading and guiding me,
Just like a miner's light does.

All around is your goodness and mercy.
All around is your beauty and bounty.
The enemy may look,
But he cannot taste Your goodness like I can.
The enemy cannot sit at Your table like I can.
He can only see from afar.

Your anointing breaks the enemy's yoke.
As you anoint me with the oil of Your Holy Spirit,
I am set free into Your abundance
Of love, life and joy.
Therefore, Your goodness and love
Will be my portion
Both now and in Heaven forever.

Amen and amen.

***

Dear Child

Life is a journey – full of ups and downs
Some days of darkness and some days of Light.

As we forgive one another and go forward,
The Light gets stronger and brighter,
The ups become more frequent and the dark days
Pushed back into the past where they belong.

Forty years into a journey may seem a long time,
But with God's Light streaming into the unblemished days
And years ahead, life can only get better and better.

I can assure you that the next forty years will be
So, so much better than the last forty.
You may ask how I know.
I know because my life has become
Radically better than my last forty years.

Yes, there will be challenges, there is no denying the fact,
But in saying that, I am confident you will go further
Into the Light as you enter into the next phase of your life.

***

Worship the Lord

As the saints of old worshipped at Your footstool
So come, let us bow in worship.

Let us kneel before the Lord our Maker.
He will bring correction. He will bring joy.
His love will cover us as we seek His face.

His joy and compassion will overtake us
As we seek His face.
He will never forsake us.
As we seek His face
We will rest in His grace.

***

My Dearest Daughter

I love you so, so much. You are extremely precious to Me. You are a beautiful flower gradually unfolding into fullness. I delight in you, and I can't keep My eyes from looking at you. I want always to look at you because you are the apple of My eye and so beautiful to behold. I appreciate your heart of worship, and I love to hear you sing to Me – your singing heart makes My heart sing. You bring Me great joy.

With regard to your journey, please be aware that I do things in My timing. I am the One who heals, and I do it in My time and in My way. In saying that, I want you to encourage and build up your mother-in-law – speak to her the Word of Faith that is in your heart – encourage her to renew her faith in Me. Her faith has gone downhill because no one is standing with her and/or alongside her in her distress. She needs building up so she can receive her healing. She needs to know that Jesus still cares for her and has not forgotten her.

Do not worry about the man at your side as he is in My hand also, and the timing for him is not yet. Be faithful to what I have taught you and the Word of Life that is in your heart.

I have made you a flower that is resilient against the wind, and I have rooted you deep into Me. This means you can stand and not be swayed by stuff that happens around you. You can be assured I am supporting and holding you secure in your faith, for it is the faith of Jesus that sustains you. My precious Son has purchased you and my precious Son's blood is what keeps you secure.

I am resolute in My determination that nothing shall snatch you from My hand and that in the fullness of time, you will be an open blossom and sending forth an even stronger fragrance of My Love to those around you.

I love you so much. You are the apple of my eye.
God the Father

***

Encouragement to a Wife

Fear not my daughter – I am in this situation, and you will come forth as gold as through the fire. I will refine, I will burn the dregs, and you will be even more beautiful in my sight.

I know where you dwell and where Satan has his throne at the moment, but I am the One who raises up and I am the One who tears down.

Keep your eyes fixed on Me. Let not your heart be troubled. Look up and live – dig deep into my strength - My well of living water – for the believing wife sanctifies the unbelieving husband – only do not let his words of condemnation and divisiveness drive you anywhere but onto your knees before Me.

You are a shining light, My daughter, and you will shine even more brightly when this season is over.

I am the Alpha and Omega, the Beginning and the End. Seasons come and seasons go, but I the Lord remain forever. I am your Rock, fall on Me – I will support you. A smoking flax I will not destroy. Put your faith and hope in Me alone and see what I will do.

***

Written for a friend with serious marriage problems

Word to the Wise

Hear, hear O My daughter – I have done great things for you
And will continue to do so.
Have you not heard, have you not seen how great I am?
I AM the I AM of all your tomorrows as well as today.
I have preserved and coveted you from the beginning.
You are who you are, and
Where I want you to be at this moment.
I am connecting the dots, so sit back and watch.
Keep your focus on Me, your Lord,
And watch Me and see Me as I weave everything together.

***

Going Home to Jesus

I hear the angels calling. They're coming to take me home,
To the splendour of His Glory, His Love, and to His Throne.
I hear the Heavenly music. It is so sweet to hear.
The throngs, and the masses, are raising up a cheer.
My appointed time is near, the door is opening wide.
I hear my Jesus calling – come here My child, abide.
I am looking forward to this time, when my earthly life is o'er.
I am looking to the beauty, of the Lord I adore.
I sense His welcome arms are open wide,
and like a little child I will run inside.

My family here on earth do dwell,
But their appointed time will come,
As each of us knows well.
And when their time shall come
To leave this earth for Heaven,
I shall be at that door –
And with Jesus at my side, will welcome them inside.
So do not fret, my children, this is just the norm.
With Jesus at your side, you will ride the storm.

Have no fear for me, I am doing well.
With Jesus by my side, I shall not enter hell.
Jesus lives in Heaven, and He has promised me
A place, purpose built, and He built it just for me.
I go now to that place of health, and life and joy
Where none can steal, or moth corrupt,
In my Eternal Home.
Peace and Joy now reign as my spirit enters in.
I am like a butterfly emerging with new wings.
So do not fret, my children, this is just the norm.
With Jesus at your side, you too, will enter in.

***

Singing a Love Song

I will sing to You a love song.
I will sing to You my praise.
For You alone have redeemed me,
And I will live for You always.

O Jesus, fount of living water.
You alone shall fill my heart.
You alone shall overflow me.
I will praise and glorify Your Name.

O Jesus, You are my love song.
You will always be my praise.
To You I give all honour. To You I sing my praise.
To You I give all honour. To You I give all praise.
To You I give all praise, and glory to Your Name.

***

The Open Door

There is an open door, a door I must walk through.
It is a door of beauty and I owe it all to You.
A door that leads to happiness, to joy, and to new life.
It is a door of promise that promises me more.
Of all the life I ever lived, it promises much more.

I see the Light behind it, which gets brighter every day.
I see my Saviour's face and know He leads the way.
I am not really frightened. I see beyond my cares,
To a life that's just beginning, if I'll only step 'out there'.
But where is there? I ask myself, as I ponder it anew.
My Saviour answers me. "Why don't you come and see,
I have made it all brand new".

I step beyond the veil, which only seeks to hide
What I have searched for all my life – to no avail.
He beckons me to come and so I enter in
To the newness of the Life, He has created from within.
'Tis new and I've not been that way before,
And yet, here I am, walking through the open door.

The open door is special. I have longed for it so much.
It's hard to tell, where I would be, without the Master's touch.
He comes to me with love, and drying all my tears,
He says "My child – I love you very much".

I now can see the sunshine, as my pain is drained away.
His loving kindness seems like gentle rain, on a summer's day.
As I lift my eyes to Heaven and I behold His face,
The Glory of His Splendour helps me run my race.
I do not race against the clock, nor against my fellow man.
I run the race in victory, with Christ, my right hand Man.

***

Whispers in the Night

In the stillness of the night,
When the stars are shining bright,
I see my Saviour seated on the Throne.
His loving gaze, I see His eyes.
He will with me abide.

I wait, as He draws the curtains back.
It is as if He sees my back.
I am all covered in the scars,
Where upon I laid my all.
He whispers, 'My child, your back
Is now like Mine. You have identified'.

My healing now will flow
O'er all that you have known.
I will make the stars so bright.
They will make your night, daylight.
So do not fear, My child of faith.
I am the One Who gives you grace.

Amen. Amen. Amen

***

Butterfly Wings

I am a little butterfly with some brand new wings.
I hear my Saviour calling, and He's calling me to sing.
What shall I sing, I ask Him, as I move my wings with care.
I'm not sure I know the song. It seems a bit 'out there'.

I know what I can do, as I survey His cross.
I'll spread my wings in gratitude and that will make a noise.
I spread my wings out wide, then bring them to my side.
I see my Saviour smiling and I find myself now gliding.

I am drawn toward His nose, and land there in repose.
A place of rest and safety as I look into His eyes
And I am reminded, of the sparrows that He knows.

What is the song that I should sing?
What is the gift that I should bring?
To be myself in Him alone
And be with Him around the throne.

The colours in my wings are bright.
They shine like stars in broad daylight.
I'll sing because I'm happy. I'll sing because I'm free.
His eye is not just on the sparrow.
His eye is directly on me.

Queen Esther

Queen Esther sat in her boudoir, all alone in thought.
Her people were not safe, as Haman planned a plot.
His plot to overthrow Queen Esther's every wish,
Was fraught with danger for the queen,
And made her wish him dead.

She thought this way and that, and tried to overcome
The fear that was encircling her, because of Haman's plot.
But now, a thought occurred, a new one, I assume.
I'll seek the presence of my God,
And on Him I will presume.

The faithful Mordecai, Esther's father figure head,
Did surely give to her, a wise and thinking head.
She thought and thought, and then a plan arose.
My maids and I will fast, so the story goes.

For three long days they fasted,
And even through the night.
There was not one, single, patty cake in sight.

The fast was over, the table laid, for king and countryman.
Haman appeared, the king retired, and so the fight began.
Long story, short, the king, found out about
The plot that Haman had planned.
His work was swift, the end had come
For Haman and all he had done.

Queen Esther stood in her beautiful dress,
A crown upon her head.
She had saved the day. Her people were free.
And now she could go to bed.

***

Morning is Here

A new chapter in my life, has only just begun.
A chapter of such grace, that the story must be spun.
'Tis a brand new morning, the dew is on the ground,
My Saviour's face is shining, from the glory all around.

I am no longer small. I have grown up quite a bit.
It seems that only yesterday, I was just a little kid.
But seasons come, and seasons go, and now that I am here,
I will enjoy myself again and I will have no fear.
The darkness of the night is so distanced from my life.
It seems a great big dream and that is quite all right.

Today, and yes, tomorrow, will be different from the past.
My joy is never ending, and it will be so vast.
For my Saviour, He has promised, to be with me, to the end.
I see His hand of mercy. I see Him as my friend.
His hand of grace and mercy will follow me again
To this land which is unending, where I will dance and sing.

I have no fear now of my past, for all the doors are shut.
My Saviour God has brought me through,
And He says, I am free.
It is His very presence, which drives the fear away.
It is His very presence, that puts the doubt at bay.
My mind, it is now clear. It is a brand new day.

The Lord is now my right hand man,
And I cannot do without, His loving kindness and attention,
Which shall be my life throughout.
His glory now is here. His presence in my midst,
He has not forgotten, that I am only dust.
His gentle loving kindness has brought me out and through
Into the sunlight of His love, as only He can do.

I hear my Saviour calling, when the night, it is far spent.
I am coming now, my Lord, and I struggle out of bed.
This time together, O so sweet.
It is the time, Jesus wants, He and I to meet.
My day is here – it has begun – to meet again with Him.
My day has zest, when He knows best,
And so to Him I run.

It is that time of day, when I am sleepy eyed.
He knows that I am rich, when with Him I abide.
His blessings are abundant and so I take them all,
Because I do not know how this day, will unfold.
The sun is shining bright. The stars have gone to sleep.
My Saviour's brightness lights my way
And I am His to keep.

I see His hand of mercy. I hear His voice of cheer.
Get up, my little darling. Your brand new day is here.
I see some new horizons, like diamonds on the ground.
It is a new beginning. It is a brand new morn,
And there are treasures to be found.

***

My Passion

It is my greatest passion, to see my Lord on high,
And yet, He died upon a cross, and this, it makes me cry.
My loving Lord, My friend so dear, was hung a way up high.
His cross was planted on a hill so high, for all to see.
It was for you, He died, and so it was for me.

His love is now transcending across the aeons of our time.
His love is everlasting to touch your heart and mine.
His love is so complete, as only time can tell
When He reaches out to you and saves you from all hell.

I have now some understanding
Of what it cost for Him to die.
And now my heart, it yearns for Him,
For He can satisfy the deepest longings of my life
And He can make me fly.

I fly to Him in my dreams, and in my waking hours.
I sense His Holy Presence, in the wee, small hours.
His love, it comes on pinions, and I am carried on His wings
To His everlasting comfort and in His presence I can sing.

My loving Saviour knows me through and through.
It is a close relationship between His heart and mine.
I long for His appearing in glory and in power
And yet, I wait, for His eternal hour.

The time, it comes, as each day passes by.
My Saviour God has promised, He will not pass me by.
I long for His appearing, not only as a guest,
But as my Lord, my Saviour, the One I worship best.

My passion now is kindled, as I wait upon my Lord.
I love to have Him present, as I meet Him all the more.
It is the loving Father who calls the sinner home.
It is the Holy Spirit, who meets me in my home.

My Saviour, Lord, my God and King,
Now reigns upon the throne.
My heart is clean, He says to me,
For He has washed me in His blood.

I await His Holy Presence, for more infilling I would seek,
The everlasting power, as I sit down at His feet.
I want to magnify, to glorify His Name,
By doing what He did, to heal the sick and lame.
It is a glorious venture, not withstanding all my fear.
It cost Him quite a lot, of that I am quite clear.

My Hero, He does ride upon a great white horse.

His mouth, it seems, is filled with the flaming sword.

He is the Word of Truth, where no lie can attend.

He is my Jesus, my Master, and my Friend.

His resurrection power now flows through all my veins.

Here I stand amazed, by the power through which He flows.

To live my life for Him – to live for Him alone.

Nothing is more significant, than to live my life in Him.

***

The House Next Door

The golden clouds are forming, and the dew is on the ground,
I see my Saviour calling with sunlight on His brow.
The Heavenly gates are open, the angels are in sight,
I see his beauty and His glory are shining in the light.
I long for His appearing, and yet, He waits for me.

This is not the grand finale, it is all an open door
As I step into His presence, because He lives next door.
The door between His house and mine was never really shut
Because we had such visits, betwixt the two of us.
And now my house is shutting up, the blinds are being drawn
As I step into my Father's house, the one He built next door.

His house, it is so very different, and nothing can compare
To the healing, health and wholeness
I shall receive when there.
It is a new dimension as only one can see, when I step across
The threshold of His house, the one He built for me.

***

Written when my friend Anita was diagnosed with cancer

Midnight to Sunshine

'Tis midnight in the day, for those who are so sick
In soul and mind and body, for whom the darkness is so thick.
I look upon myself and ponder all my past.
This is what it looked like, as I breathed my last.
I could not comprehend, where day or night, it was.
All that I could think of, was how to make it pass.
I pondered all the time, why things were, as they were,
And yet, in my small mind, something was astir.

I couldn't figure out, just what was going on,
But Someone took my hand, and then I just moved on
Into some sunlight, into the Light of day.
I knew I had arrived, into some understanding,
Which cannot be denied.
I am loosed, I cried, as I crossed to the other side.
The darkness is no more.

In the sunlight of His presence, I can now abide.
The Lord, He is so good to me. I shall ne'er forget
The day He took my hand, and said, 'let us ever
Forget, the past of darkness and of pain.
It is a new tomorrow. It is a brand new day'.

I am living now with Him. My days are ever bright.
I never thought I'd see the day, where everything is Light.

My family here on earth do dwell.
Their hearts are heavy, as I know very well.
I could not live my life in hell, and so with Jesus I now dwell.
Jesus knows my heart, as much as He knows yours,
But He offered me an open door through which I must depart.
My life, it is important, and so it is with those I leave behind.
I say to you, do not let your grief overwhelm you all the time.
I am now with Jesus, and yes, I am fine.
There is no darkness where He is – it is all sunshine.

The beauty of His Presence, the sunshine of His day,
It has already come and dried my tears away.
So do not fret my loved ones, as you go through the fray.
I know I shall see you all again, in the sunshine, on that day
When you step into Glory and see the Son arise.

It is so pleasant over here. My eyes, they are so bright.
I look forward to seeing you,
When you step through that Light.
I cannot imagine how you will look,
When we greet each other again.
I only know, when you get here, there will be no more pain.

There will be laughter, and hugs all around,
And tears are drained away,
For the sunshine of His loving Presence encircles us each day.

This was written for a family whose son suicided

***

Tears are Raining

There seems to be a difference
Between the sunshine and the rain.
The rain, it brings some heartache, and even can bring gain.
I sometimes wonder about the time,
This rainfall, it should come.
It seems I cannot worry, about that which is not done.
It is as if the lightening comes,
Straight through my broken heart.
I want to know, what is the wrong that I have done?

'Tis nothing wrong, my Lord replies,
As He brings His comfort near.
I just check to see, if you can feel, My ever aching heart.
My heart, it is so tender. I want to share My pain.
My people do not realize, I am in the falling rain.
The falling rain, it seems, are some of Jesus' tears
Which fall upon the earth, on those with all their fears.

The hardness of the heart – the latitude of pain,
It seems so, never ending, and so the tears began.
My Jesus, He is so soft of heart, and I must be that way
To heal the broken hearted and bring them into gain.

To be like Jesus is my goal – it is my aim, my creed.
To be like Him in everything – to be like Him always.

His love is like the sunshine, which dries up all our tears,
And yet amid the sunshine, He has to calm our fears.
We need to recognize, that the sunshine and the rain
Are all a part of Jesus' love, and He has come to reign
Upon our hearts, to soften and to quell,
The heaviness of spirit which some of us know well.

His rain, it begins to soak, into the dryness of our lives.
The only thing that satisfies, the deepest, driest well.
Our tears, they well up, as the rain begins to fall,
For Jesus, He brings life, where there was no life at all.

***

Precious Moments

I have some precious moments I spend alone with Him.
I have some special memories, from where it all began.
My memory bank is full, of moments, pure and sweet,
Of times alone with Jesus, when often we would meet.
These times, they are so precious, some fleeting, others long.
But time alone with Jesus, is what gives to me my song

I do not crave the world, and its pleasures which look sweet.
I crave the moments with my Lord, so He my soul will keep.
My soul, it wasn't very well, as anyone could tell.
Then Jesus came along, His love, so pure and clean,
He has done all things well, and made me just like Him.

My soul, it is now happy, my soul, is it now clean.
For Jesus washed me in His blood,
And He has made me whole.
My precious moments now do have, a whole new story line
Of love and mercy, grace and peace. To Him I am aligned.

***

Shadows of the Night

It is the shadow of the night that makes my heart so weary.
In the morning hours, I find myself quite teary.
But tears, they do not flow when I am fast asleep.
They only manifest as I choose my soul to keep.
The Lord He is so good to Me. He keeps my heart alive.
He wants to bring me healing, so I don't have to, just survive.
It is His blessing to me, to keep the night away,
But memories, unconscious, assail my soul all day,
And the night is like the darkness,
That my soul has e'er known long.

The morning light is shining, like sunbeams in my day,
But the shadows of the night want to chase the sun away.
I choose to live for Jesus. He is my all in all.
I choose to live for Jesus. He is my open door
To all I have believed in, and all I am believing for.
The night, it is far spent, but my grieving heart does know
The shadow of the night still seems to overflow.

I want the sun to shine and chase the dark away.
I am sure that this will happen, as I yield to Him this day,
For Jesus is the Light and no power of hell can stay.

His Word says, He alone, sends the darkness far away.
I come now to His Light, the Brightness of the day,
To succour and to triumph in this, His Glorious Day.
I shall not fear the battle, but face it with a grin.
I am an overcomer, through Jesus Christ, the King.

My soul has been so tortured. My soul is still in pain.
The pain my Saviour bore, when on Him my sins were lain.
That cross upon a lonely hill was where He died for me.
'Tis where the shadows of His night were there for all to see.
My shadows, they are shrinking. My shadows, they are less,
As more and more to Jesus, I give my soul to bless.

The nail prints in His hands, the sword thrust through His side
Only make me wonder, at how my Lord did die.
His very soul was tortured by the taunting in His day.
His body hung upon the cross to take my sin away.
His shadows are not like mine. His shadows brought an end
To life and limb upon that cross, so that I could sing,
And yet my singing comes and goes along with all my pain.
I long to see the day when I can fully sing again.

To sing is so much nicer than living with the pain
Which creates some havoc, as I seek to rise again
From the shadows of the past, which so want to live today.

These shadows want to take my joy, but my Saviour
He has died. He did gain the victory, and so must I.
The torture of the past, which all hell it did impart,
Is swallowed by His resurrection, and my soul is set apart.
My freedom, it is here. My freedom, it will stay,
For My Saviour God has washed my pain away.

The shadows of the night are like a sounding bell
Which keeps on ringing,
Even though the ringer has been quelled.
I will lift my eyes to Heaven, and so to Him I cry,
"It's over – it's time for shadows to go,
And it's time for me to live."
My Jesus, He does all things well,
And that my soul knows indeed.
He takes the shadows of my night and throws them into hell.
The morning now has broken, the sunbeams come again.
I pray the Lord my soul to keep, and I begin to sing.

***

Angels of the Realm

The angels are so real. They are around us every day.
Do you feel their gentle touch?
Do you sense their beauty and their worth
As you go about your day?
Or does your very attitude push them far away?

For angels have a purpose in the realm of God.
He sends them to their duties,
As our prayers to God we raise.
Some are flaming ones, and others dressed in white.
Some have beautiful wings, and some do not.
It just all depends on God.

Have you felt the angel wings touching you this day?
Know your prayers are being answered
By His angels sent to you today.
For God sends His Holy angels, His messengers of fire,
To assist those being saved, and to bring them out of mire.

Look for the angels in your life,
The ones who do you good.
For God looks down from Heaven
And sees your need today.
And then He commands some angels,
To help you on your way.

***

Reign of Love

His sunshine and His rain now comes to me again.
The sunshine is His Light, and His Spirit is the rain.
His rain, it is now falling, washing me anew.
It is to build me up, and to make me all brand new.

I am like that little spider that climbs the water spout.
I keep on, keeping on, even though I am washed out.
My life has been so drained by misadventure's turn.
It is the Holy Spirit Who keeps filling up my urn.

His love is like the sunshine. It brightens up my day.
The gentle rain of Heaven is what keeps me here today.
I long for His appearing. He is my dearest friend.
I know Him as my Jesus, my Saviour, and my King.

I love to walk with Jesus and He loves to walk with me.
We have so much in common – it is communion sweet.
We share each other's day and share each other's tears.
It is because of this, He takes away my fears.

He is my dearest friend on whom I can rely.
He alone keeps my secrets and keeps them safe always.
His love is like the rainbow, which wraps me all around.
The colour and the beauty, in none other can be found.

I do not claim to know all things, but one thing I do know
Is that Jesus is a friend who keeps, and the lover of my soul.
My soul, it is now happy. My soul, it now can sing.
My soul, it now can rest, for Jesus gives the best.

The days of war are over, with Jesus by my side.
He has won the victory, and I will now abide
In the peace and tranquillity, that He alone provides.
His provision is so great, that I can hardly wait to enter
Into His wider circle, and share this with His people.
They are so starved of love through misadventure's turn.
So what I have, I give to them, so they may be the urn
The Holy Spirit fills, when it becomes their turn.

***

My 'Get up and Go'

My 'get up and go' it is far spent.
It went through the night and didn't come back.
But my Jesus says to me, Follow Me.
His 'get up and go' will be my strength, so says He.

My night was long, o'er many years,
And sunshine did not shine.
But now the night is shattered, and I'm no longer bound.
My 'get up and go' was a long time ago,
But Jesus says, I will be with you, wherever you go.

How do I get it back, I ask, as I leave the scene.
It is a new tomorrow, a sight I have not seen.
My 'get up and go', it will return with the new day,
But somehow, I suspect, it will never be the same.

My Jesus now, is all in all, as King David did attest,
If I had not had the conflict, I would not know His rest.
His rest is what will give me, all the 'go' I'll ever need.
To follow His heart, with all my heart, will give a new start.

My 'get up and go' I cannot find, as I begin this day.
My walk with Jesus will somehow, restore to me
My zest for life, my passion, to live for Him today.
I do not understand how He can do this just for me.

Upon a lonely hill, He on a cross did bear
All my sin and iniquity, and yet, He just stayed there.
His passion for me, it did not die, only His earthly shell,
And yet, for me was crucified, to keep me out of hell.

His 'get up and go' was all snuffed out,
As He died upon that cross.
All of hell, it did not know,
He would rise up to become the Boss.

His 'get up and go' it did rise, on that Easter Sunday morn.
All hell awoke, so forlorn, their 'get up and go' was gone.
For Jesus, He did conquer the mastermind behind
My night of terror and of fear, which started long ago.

The new day is so bright, with promises all around.
It is a day, I'm sure, when my 'get up and go' is found.
For Jesus, He has promised to be with me to the end.
I have no lack of confidence in Jesus as my friend.

It might be a slow beginning as the season turns around.
The night is gone, the day is here - new zest for life appears.
The 'get up and go' I once did have, is nowhere to be found.
It died a painful death, and I am born again with tears.

The old is gone, the new has come. I know where I have been,
And now I am headed, into some realms unseen.
These realms are vast with joys untold, and as I tell the tale,
My 'get up and go' is now restored,
At the sound of Jesus Name.

***

Children from the Nest

My children from the nest have flown.
The time has gone – it is so long
Since they gave their hearts to Him
And wandered somewhere down the road
To other places, sights and sounds.

The Lord, He is so good. The Lord He is so true.
He will bring them back to Him
And they will come home, too.
I feel like I am looking down a long and dusty road.

My son is so long coming. He is on a gravelled road.
The road he treads is tricky and he slips and slides at will,
But Jesus is still there and extends His hand to him, until
My son, he sees it, and grabs it with his own.
I cannot force my son, to take the Master's hand.
I can only hope and pray, he sees that outstretched hand.

My daughter is so different. Her life is not sublime,
And so she put some distance, between her heart and mine.
She left the nest, to escape, the trauma in her life.
To my chagrin, I found, the trauma did rebound.

It came back to bite me hard, is all that I can say.
But Jesus came to help me, as I prayed for her that day.
My daughter now, she speaks to me
And sometimes from her heart.
And yet, I do not know her. We are a thousand miles apart.

Jesus, He has promised, my family, they are His.
His ever loving arms will gather them right in,
And then one day, we all shall be restored.

My children, they will come and nest with me again.
This coming time is different, and not the same as then.
We each will make our way, to the cross
Which takes our sins away.
There will be forgiveness, on every side, I'm sure,
As my children come on home, and nest with me once more.

***

First Fruits

My father is the first fruits of those returning to the fold.
He is the head of family and brings a wealth untold
Of loving kindness in abundance, which he just needs to share
With those who are returning,
From their journey way out there.

He has paved the way for others who would come
To my home in the country, and to the Blessed Son.
For Jesus, He did promise me that all my family
Would, one by one, come and live near me.

My dad has always been, stuck in a type of warp.
His future now secured as he maintains his walk
With Jesus as his Leader, his Helper and his Guide.
A little bit like Abraham – with Jehovah by his side.

For many a year, my dad has been in his lowly abode.
With no family by his side, it seems he has been slowed.
And now the opportunity presents, a lifestyle change, no less,
To move himself and his goods, to a new place of rest.

I pray this move, it will be good for him to see
Other people of his age and of some new society.
To move into a world where he is not confined,
And limited only to himself, and those he leaves behind

There is a whole new world awaiting dad,
As he trembles at the thought
Of leaving a life, of so many years, at the same resort.
But places come, and places go, as time, it marches on.
The only place dad needs today, is a place to hang his hat on.

My family will soon gather, together with my dad.
The prodigals are returning, for they, by the Lord are stirred
To return to the fold, of family, kith and kin.
Dad and I will welcome them and quietly bring them in.

Our hearts will be rejoicing as we enter into spring.
The Lord Himself is gathering all the wanderers in.
The Lord Himself, He knows, all the pain we have been in
As the children, they have wandered,
From dry spring to dry spring.

Now is the time to set our hearts aglow,
To see the fruit of all our prayers,
Even though there's just a hint, of changes in the air
And fragrance on the breeze,
We know that God is in the background
Tying up loose ends with ease.

Our new tomorrow is almost here.
The wanderers are coming home.
The joy within our hearts will soon enough resound
At the sound of laughter, love, and happiness
As again we are a family, newly found.

Praise be to God on High. Praise be to His Son,
Praise be to the Holy Spirit.
The Glorious Godhead, three in one.

Amen. Amen. Amen.

***

Dreams for Eternity

The Lord, He is my Shepherd. I know I shall not want.
His very Presence, He does fill me up with love.
I know Him as my Saviour among other names of His,
But now I have a new name, Sustainer of all things.

He is my all in all and I will follow Him where He leads,
Because where He leads, He feeds.
He is feeding me His joy. He is feeding me with love.
His peace is bubbling up, and that is what I need.

My new tomorrow now is here. This day it has begun.
The ups and downs of yesterday have gone, never to return.
My new day, it is where my Lord's promises are fulfilled.
I am looking forward to when all my dreams come true.

My dream of family once again coming through my door.
My dream of living undisturbed by God's own golden shore.
My dream of giving Gospel words that ring out loud and clear.
My dream of seeing multitudes come to the Jesus I adore.
My dream to heal the broken hearted,
And set the captive free.
My dreams are now within my reach and soon will be reality.

I have no claim to fame, or fortunes in the bank.

I only have my Jesus – it is He Who fills my tank.

I am like a little teapot – Jesus fills me up,

And then I pour Him out.

***

Risen Triumphant

It was my Lord Who died for me.
Crucified upon a tree.
It was my Lord Who set me free.
It was my Lord on Calvary.

He is risen. Christ is risen.
He has conquered sin and darkness.
He is risen. Christ is risen.
Glory be to God on High.

It was my Lord Who suffered pain.
It is my Lord Who lives again.
He rose again to live for me.
He rose from that accursed tree.

He is risen. Christ is risen.
He has conquered sin and darkness.
He is risen. Christ is risen.
Glory be to God on High.

My Lord, He sits upon a throne,
Highly exalted in Heaven above.
My Lord, He reigns as King on High
So you and I can be satisfied.

He is risen. Christ is risen.
He has conquered sin and darkness.
He is risen. Christ is risen.
Glory be to God on High.

He is risen, the Bible says.
His foes are gone to hell's hot flames.
The Lord is King o'er all the earth.
The Lord is King – over death.

He is risen. Christ is risen.
He has conquered sin and darkness.
He is risen. Christ is risen.
Glory be to God on High.

My Lord has triumphed over sin.
His love has brought the sinners in.
My Saviour God has ransomed me.
My Saviour God will set you free.

He is risen. Christ is risen.

He has conquered sin and darkness.

He is risen. Christ is risen.

Glory be to God on High.

Glory be to God on High.

Glory be to God on High.

***

Pentecost is Coming

My Jesus, He was crucified upon a tree,
And I know He did it just for me.
He rose again that early morn,
And so in me, His love was born.

Now Pentecost is almost here.
Those friends of His were gripped by fear.
They did not know, on that day,
That the power of God would come their way.
This power, it would equip them to do what Jesus did,
To preach the word –
heal the sick and even raise the dead.

Now in this day and age, some people, they would scoff.
They would say it's stupid, and laugh it all right off.
But Jesus is consistent with the time frame that He has.
He is no man's debtor and so His love reflects.

It's time for Him to come again in power, as He did of old.
For Pentecost is almost here in this day and hour.
I long for the appearing of His Holy Ghost.

It's fire I want, for fire I plead – the fire of His Pentecost.
I want His Pentecost of fire for me.

His fire will empower me to live as I should live
In my local city, and then beyond the sea.
To witness of His grace to those who are so lost.
To heal the sick, to raise the dead, and to endure the cost.

His fire, it has begun to fall on those who want to see,
The Majesty and Glory, of Christ, our Saviour King.
Soon it will arrive in the fullness of His time.
Our open hearts are ready to receive Him as Divine.
His power will overflow us, and our lives,
They will be changed in an instant of time,
As the fire of Pentecost falls again.

***

Dad's Move

My father, he is packing, to go to his new home.
There are many things in boxes and many still to come.
His love of God above will hold him in good stead
For when he moves, he will lose, some friends of his so dear.
But coming up, in his new home, are friends he's never met.

These friends of his will not be lost, and never will be gone,
For they are on the telephone and not so far away.
His new friends, they will live, next door or across the way.
He only has to smile at them and say, "the kettle's on".
Then he will find the welcome mat will not go far astray.

People love to have a cuppa, as good friends usually do.
They sit, relax, and chat about just what is going on.
The people in the village are so kind and good and true.
But it seems that God has planned Dad's life to be renewed.
But now a challenge has been set, to start his life anew.

The packing is now nearly done and the garden it looks poor,
As plants are being packaged up to put near Dad's new door.
These plants, they will remind him, that life is still so green
In the country, where the air it is so clean.
For Dad will start a new and different life of which we all agree.

Although all bridges are not crossed, Dad is on his way,
To a life of difference from the one he knows this day.
A life we hope will bring enrichment,
Of joy and love and peace.
A life of satisfaction which brings forth no more tears,
A life of family and of friends, to fill his lasting years.

***

Now hope does not disappoint, because the love of God has been poured out in our hearts by the Holy Spirit who was given to us.

Romans 5:5 NKJV

Brian

I can see my friend Brian. He is walking down the street.
His head is held up high. There is sunshine on his feet.
He has a purpose, I would say, from the way he looks today.
I sense he has a meeting with Someone on the way.

This Someone, I am sure, is looking for him too.
And by the sound of things, their meeting will ensure
A change of life and of pose,
Toward the One, Brian did oppose.
I have met this One before, and I am very sure
Brian's outlook will be changed,
Once Jesus breaks the chains.

The chains of darkness got a hold, long before Brian got old.
But Jesus has the power, and it seems to be the hour
When these chains, they must fall off.
The Light has come. The day has dawned,
And Brian's whole life will be reformed.

Brian's wife of many years
Has offered up her heartfelt prayers,
And sometimes through the night,
Her prayers are mixed with tears.
Now Jesus, He is ready to answer all the prayers.
His timing, it is perfect, and will roll away the fears.

Brian's new found faith in Christ alone,
Will hold him in good stead,
As he sets his eyes on Jesus,
The Glory, and the Lifter of his head.
And Brian's new life, it will bring,
Praises to our Heavenly King.
And all of Heaven, it will shout,
Praise to God who got him out.

***

What is Truth?

What is truth? The man, he asked.
I see the earth, the skies, and seas,
Surely there is truth in these.
I see the cattle in the field.
Their innards will the truth reveal.
I throw some stones upon the ground.
In them I see the truth is found.
But what is truth? he asks again,
For I am lost and I am bound.
Bound by what? I ask the man.
Bound by selfishness, and greed,
And powers unseen upon me feed.

I looked the man straight in the eye.
It seems to me, he wants to die.
And yet, there is a longing to be free.
To hope in something he does not see.
So now I speak – The Truth is not a what,
But Who. Do you see?
He looked at me in disbelief, and said,
Can this Person really see, all I am cut out to be?
Yes, I say, He surely can,

If only to Him you would come.
He will wash your sins away.
He will change your night to day.
He has broken the powers of hell.
My Jesus has done all things well.

The man, he looked surprised
At the Name of Jesus Christ.
He did not know that Truth was He,
Who died upon that cruel tree.
He had not heard of Jesus' power,
To break the chains of unseen powers,
Nor Jesus' power to quell all fear,
And heal the sick this very hour.

Then I met another man,
Who had heard the Saviour's Name,
But he did not believe,
And from science did receive
What he perceived to be the truth.
And when he hugged some great big tree,
He said, he knew, this truth, it was for him.

But, alas, the tree, it did not give him help.
The tree just stood there on a hill.

For trees do raise their arms up high,
Proclaiming majesty to God Most High.
And so, this man, he is lost.
He does not want to know the cross
Which leads him to the Truth, the Who,
And not the what.

I looked this man straight in the eye.
It seems to me he just denies,
And yet, there is longing to be free,
To belong to One he does not see.
Again I speak – the Truth is not a what,
But Who. Can't you see?
He looked at me disdainfully,
And then he just reiterates
His faith in science and in trees.
And at this point I am in tears.

The man, he is surprised, I would
So bluntly tell the story of my Jesus,
Who has done all things well;
Of how the Truth has set me free and given me
Such liberty from fear and pain and hell.
I have a life free from guilt,
As now on Jesus, my life is built.

The Truth, He was revealed to me,
So now I seek Him passionately
With all my heart, my soul, my strength.
For Jesus has a plan, to save all kith and kin.
He is the Truth, the Way, the Life,
And He is not a what.
For Truth is a Person, and He is my Saviour God.

***

On Angels' Wings

My son, he is coming – borne on angels' wings.
He doesn't know it yet, but life, it is changing.
His son, he will soon be healed, of all things wrong with him,
And so, my son will reel, and then come back to me.

He will be asking questions, about just what did take place
When his child comes home, healed, from all of his disgrace.
It will surprise us all, even though it is expected.
But my son, does not know, that this is God's objective.

To bring my children home, along with all their heirs
Into the bosom of the Father, so the story fares.
The promises I have, they will be fulfilled
As my Jesus, He goes out, to do His blessed will.

My son, he is coming – borne on angels' wings
To seek a new horizon – to seek the King of Kings.
My son, he has no comprehension of what's in store that day.
But I will shout with joy and say, 'my God has won the day.'

***

The Lord is Come!

The Lord has just arrived. I see Him from my place.
He has taken all my shame and all of my disgrace.
He is coming now towards me,
With loving kindness in His hand.
He is coming to restore me, to His glorious plan.
I see His hand of mercy. I see His loving eyes.
I see His star and crown, shining in the skies.

The Lord, He is so good to me. His favour is so great.
With His hand upon me, I shall never fail to gain
All the splendour of His grace, again and again.
To bless my Lord, this is my creed, after all He's done for me.
This very day, this very hour, My Lord is on the scene.
He comes to me in glory, and in His power unseen.

The Lord comes to fulfil my dreams, as on Him I wait.
I hope in faith – I wait and wait – now He's at the gate.
He will unlock the gate that has held me in so long,
For His promises are sure, and I keep knocking on His door.

The Word says, He is knocking too, and so
Agreement has been reached,
And the door once shut - is now breached.
Now I in Him and He in me.

The Lord, He comes in splendour,
With 10,000 times 10,000 angels by His side.
He comes to set me free, as I in Him abide.
He comes to bring to me,
My family that on earth do dwell.
He restores relationship, which was lost so long ago.
He unites us into Him, as once again we come,
To his loving arms and heart,
Which welcomes us all in.

***

The Sanctuary

There are some people coming here,
Whom the Lord has taught to fear
His Holy Name, and His Presence, when He is near.
This reverential fear of God Most High,
Will bring His Name down here, quite nigh.
And when the Lord does visit us, as on bended knee we pray,
His Holy Presence fills the room, and we do want to stay.

We love His Holy Presence, for with Him we commune.
We love to sing to him, right across the room.
We fill the room with praise, as our arms to Heaven we raise
In worship of our Heavenly King, enthroned in us this day.
His Holy Presence, He does come into our midst today
And does impart, His love, His gifts.
His very Self, He gives away.

We do not know the way, the Lord He comes today.
We only know, we asked Him to visit us again.
And now He has arrived, His presence fills the place
When we come, one by one, to seek His saving grace.
The joy, He does bestow, it sets us all aglow
And I am reminded of a Sanctuary long ago.

This Sanctuary stood in a desert place,
And the singers sang His praise.
The priests, they could not stand to make the offering,
Because the Holy Cloud and Fire just filled the whole place in.
The Holiness of God, the Father, Son and Holy Ghost
Have come again to visit us in this time and place,
And our hearts are ready, to look into His face.

Our little sanctuary here on earth, is ready for the Lord.
We invited Him to come, as He passed along this way.
Our little group is pleased to have Him in this place
As we go forward, to step into His warm embrace.
The Father, Son and Holy Ghost are always welcome here,
And we to Him, will yield our hearts,
As His Presence draws us near.

***

My Friend Anita

My friend Anita is going to be married, as far as I can tell.
She marries One she loves, and He loves her as well.
Her wedding dress is beautiful as she walks up the aisle.
Her dress is purest white, with rare pearls on each side.
This dress, it was provided by her King of Kings.
It is His marriage, and a love song He does sing.

My friend Anita is going into another land
Which flows with milk and honey,
And where joy does abound.
There is no sickness there,
In that land which shines so bright.
The dress, so purest white, is reflecting all the light.
The banquet table, it is set, the angels are around.
The marriage now begins, and joybells do resound.

Anita is crossing over into a land so fair,
Away from the drudgery of life,
Which she found so hard to bear.
And even though she faced life with a grin,
It was Jesus in her heart, who took away her sin.

The wedding day has come.
The bride has now been dressed
To meet the Bridegroom in the sky,
Where she will be most blessed.

One day, we will meet again, when my turn comes around
To be dressed in purest white, in my wedding gown.
When the Lord shall call me home to His marriage feast,
And the angels shall rejoice, and the joybells never cease.

***

This poem is about my friend's impending death.

Jesus and the Snake

My Jesus, He is good, at dealing with some stuff
That was caused by the snake, hidden in the rough.
The snake, it thought, it was so good,
Until my Jesus, upon him stood.
The snake and its head were really crushed
By the One Who died upon the cross.
Who rose again to take away our world of pain.

The snake, it would slither through the grass so green
Causing havoc, e'er it went along the ground unseen.
But Jesus, He did notice, just how the snake would weave
Itself into the people's lives to make them so deceived.
Then Jesus, He decided to take on that fierce-some foe,
By doing life, upon the earth, beginning from go to whoa.

The snake did try to kill the Saviour, beginning at His birth,
But missed Him by a mile, and so did start the mirth
As Jesus and the snake, a game of cat and mouse did play.
The snake could not accomplish his evil master plan,
For Jesus did outsmart him, even though it caused Him pain.
And now the snake, his head so crushed, is in the frying pan.

One day, the frying pan will go into the fires below,
And as the snake goes with the pan, Christ alone will stand
For all the world to see, as King of Kings, and Lord of Lords;
As Ruler of the Heavens above, and Ruler of the earth below.
Then it will occur, that people far and wide
Will know without a doubt, that Jesus is alive!

***

Heavenly Bliss

My friend Anita has been married to the One she loves.
Her husband's name is Jesus and He lives in Heaven above.
Her every move is now with ease – her life complete at last.
She did so very much, in what is now her past.

Her Saviour, Jesus, was her friend. On Him she did rely,
And she with Him walked hand in hand until life's very end.
And yet, life has not ended. It has only just begun.
For what is 74 years, when there are thousands yet to come.

Anita left a legacy which is long lasting and is true.
Her prayers stacked one on one, for family, me and you.
She is the seed planted in the ground just as her Jesus was.
He is risen and so is she. Now the seed will grow.

The Lord does water all her prayers,
As He does yours and mine.
He knows the beginning from the end,
And the race we each must run.

He knew Anita's pain, in her body and her soul.
He knew she wanted freedom,
And so He took her home.

You and I are blessed to have called Anita friend.
We, like her, must run our race until the very end.
One day, we too, will marry our best friend.
His Name is Jesus, and He loves us to the end.

The wedding feast is ready. The table, it is set.
Heavenly bliss is waiting for us to enter in.
Jesus is our Bridegroom. He has prepared the way.
Just say 'yes' to Jesus. I want to follow Him.
And like Anita, you will find, a place in Heaven for you.

***

Written after Anita died

The Man of My Dreams

The man of my dreams – O where can I find him?
His long flowing locks – black as a raven.
His armour, bright and shining – his steed so well groomed.

The man of my dreams – the one I have married
The one who gives life to my dreams
He is the one my heart loves – the one whose heart loves me.

The man of my dreams – the one I live with
The one who listens to my cares and my joys
The one my heart cares for –
The one with whom I laugh and cry.

The man of my dreams – the one with the dancing eyes
The one who knows my foibles and yet still adores me
The one who makes me feel welcome.

The man of my dreams – how I bless him
He is a worthy man – a man of honour
Thanks be to God Who gave me, the man of my dreams.

***

My Prayer

My grandson, he is waiting for me to pray for him
Some healing in his heart – some healing in his head.
For he is broken hearted, and his head, it is not right.
I pray I have the chance to pray for him this night.

This child who is so precious – the eldest one I have
Is living proof, of where my prayers they need to go.
For Jesus is the answer to every question that I have
Of what, and how, and why, and when.

So, as I lay me down to sleep, I do not ask my soul to keep.
I ask for one much younger, who needs your healing hand
To heal his broken heart – to help him understand –
To fix his head, so he can be, a witness to Your Majesty.

I ask a lot, O Lord, I know, but You alone can show
The power that You have, to heal this child of Yours.
A child who longs to fit, and to know his Daddy loves him so.
For me it seems, to do this, would make Your Glory overflow.

***

Blessed be the God and Father of our Lord Jesus Christ, who according to His abundant mercy has begotten us again to a living hope through the resurrection of Jesus Christ from the dead.

1 Peter 1:3 NKJV

Daddy's Little Princess

She is my little princess, and I want her just to know,
How adoringly beautiful she is, as I hold her in my arms.
But most of all, she needs to hear just how I love her so.
Her heart is clean and pure. Her longings are just fine.
I wish to tell her O so much, I think she is divine.
My little girl, with a heart of gold,
I think you're the best in all the world.

Your Daddy loves you so - I hear it loud and clear.
Your Daddy loves you so - I see it in the sky.
Your Daddy loves you so - I breathe it on the breeze.
Your Daddy loves you so - And yet, deep down.......

I struggle to believe He loves me, when awful things abound.
This and that is going wrong. My life is such a mess.
Why doesn't Daddy intervene and deal with all the bits?
He puts His arm around me and gently says to me,
Circumstances do not change the way I love you so.
Things will turn out right, just keep your eyes on Me.

Daddy can be trusted. Daddy has my hand.
Daddy knows all things and Daddy knows the end.
He could just use His arm to sweep away the mess,
And I know, He wants me to progress.

My Daddy holds my hand, and my Daddy knows my name.
I need to learn just how He does things, so I can do the same.

He says, I am His little princess, but I don't feel like that.
I am just so mixed up. I don't know who I am.
My Daddy says, you are My little princess,
And I want you just to know
Your heart of hearts is lovely, and I love you so.

My Son, He died upon the cross, a time, not long ago.
He was loved and crucified, and heartache came to Me.
So my little princess, I will help you come right through,
To a place of knowing Me.
A place which is brand new. A place of helping others
Going through what you've been through.

You are MY little princess!!!!!!!

***

The Home Coming

My daughter is coming home, and it scares me to the core.
She is coming home after years of what's gone on before.
I know that it is time for restoration to occur,
But how do I react when she comes through the door?

I know I should embrace her in love and kindness true,
But somehow, in my heart of hearts, I have some fear too.
It's been so long since things
Were right between the two of us.
It's such a shame offense took place, to drive us far apart.

But God alone knows the pain, caused by another's sin.
That sin destroyed our family and now we must begin
To mend the fences, make them straight,
And face things with a grin.
All my tears and all my prayers have risen up again.

I wonder how my daughter will view her mother,
When we meet each other.
I am not the same as twenty years ago.
I have become unknown, to the girl who left my home,
And the girl is now a woman,
With thoughts and fears of her own.

O Lord my God, please help me. I don't know where to turn
As the day approaches, when my daughter shall return.
I know that you have promised, many years ago,
To restore her to her rightful place within our home.

The day is fast appearing, with fourteen days to go.
I need to bless her through and through and cover her in love.
My ring, some new clothes, and shoes upon her feet.
I trust, my God, You will approve, the day we come to meet.

Today, O Lord my God. I will give thanks to You, forever.

It is now five days later and my daughter, she does leave.
It has been so long coming and now she must return.
However, things are not the same as they were before.
She is wrapped in love, and in love she will return to me
Like a homing pidgeon that sits upon a tree.

I thank You, Lord, for this time I could invest.
It is much sweeter now between us, but still I cannot rest.
This is a new beginning, betwixt my daughter and myself.
The journey, it has started for restoration, full and free.
The promise of my God, which He did give to me.

***

The Race

The race is not to the swift or strong.
It is to those, who to Jesus belong.
It is for all our length of days,
And we, to Him, will bring our praise.

It is a time of reflection clear,
When we bring to Him all that is dear.
It is for us to be pure and clean,
Allowing Him, ourselves to redeem.

The race keeps us running toward the goal
Of mastery over self, and self-control.
It is the time we spend in prayer
Giving to God, all of our care.

The race is not to the swift or strong,
Or we would end up, headlong
Into a mess, a miry clay,
And that would mean we had lost our way.

The race is to those who in Jesus do trust.
The race, it does cost, however, we must
Keep to the path the Lord has set,
And to follow His leading is the best bet.

The race, it will finish, when Jesus we meet.
He calls it a day, when over the line
His hand is extending, to bring us His greeting.

'Well done' He says, 'You have faithfully run
The race of your life, and now it is done.
Come into My Home you faithful one,
And wear the crown that you have won.

You are so precious in my sight,
And you are My pure delight.
The race is over, the day is done.
Now enter My Rest, blest child of God'.

***

The Door

An open door, my Saviour, He does offer me,
To come and visit Him, as He sets me free.
But the door into my life, what shall I say of it?
Will I keep it closed, or shall I open it?

The King, He is now knocking on my heart's closed door.
Should I let Him in, or will I just withdraw?
What will be the consequence of opening up to Him,
And what position will I take as I crouch behind the door?

The King, He is so patient. The King, He is Divine,
But I know this heart of mine does anything but shine.
I need His goodness and His grace to fill my days with joy.
I need His presence dearly, to feel His warm embrace.

I will take a peek to see my Lord Divine,
And as I do, I see His Majesty, so fine.
Am I worthy? I ask myself as I look into His face.
'Open up My child, and I will fill your space'.

The door, it opens, as I turn the handle from inside.
'Come in, my Lord, why do You wait outside?'
The Lord, He takes a step. A gentleman is He.
He does not override me, nor come against my will.

I have been longing for this moment, and now that it is here,
I will enjoy His presence, away from all the fear.
The tears that I have cried in pain and suffering
Are falling now like rain to make me whole again.

The door is now open. Into His presence I can come.
But Jesus stays with me, so I don't have to visit Him.
He lives in me day by day, and our fellowship is sweet.
Life is so much better since Jesus came to me.

***

A Dedication Prayer

Lord, this child whom You have given me
Is full of wonder and of grace.
I pray my Lord, his soul to keep
So he grows up to know what's right.

I pray his life is sure and sound
So grace may all the more abound.
I pray his feet be sure and strong
To stand upon the Word of God.

I pray Your Light upon his path
To light the way to You.
I pray his hands would help the lost
As he divides the Word of Truth.

I pray for me, that I may be
An example of Your Love.
To lead this child you've given me
To the Heart of God above.

***

To Him and Him Alone

I give my life to Him, the One upon the Throne.
I give my life so small, to the One Who is so tall.
I give myself to Him and Him alone.

I give myself to Him, for He gave His all for me.
I give my whole life to Him, not just a smattering.
I give myself to Him and Him alone.

I give my soul to Him, and I hear Him call my name.
I give my joy to Him, and I hear the sweet refrain.
I give myself to Him and Him alone.

I bring my tithe to Him, and the blessings they do flow.
I bring my cares to Him, for my tears they overflow.
I give myself to Him and Him alone.

I bring my heart to Him, and His heart He gives to me.
I bring my deepest thoughts, and He listens carefully.
I give myself to Him and Him alone.

O Lord my God, my Saviour, my Prophet, Priest and King.
If e'er there was one like You - an offering I would bring.
But You alone are God and there is none like You.
So I give myself to You and to You alone.

***

Follow the Star

What is that on yonder star? Yes, I see it from afar.
I see a vision clear and great, which only God,
The happening can make.

I see this vision in my dreams,
When all the world to Him would come.
I see I have small parts to play
To bring Him honour on that day.

I see the star so brightly lit. It's calling me to follow it.
I follow on to Bethlehem,
Where Christ is born the King of Kings.
The King, He is so regal. The King, He is so real.
For Jesus is the King, and at His feet I kneel.

The world, it does not come to worship at His feet
And yet, one by one, His star, they must meet.
The brightness of His coming, the Glory of that day,
When yonder Star becomes the Light that everyone shall see.

My dreams and visions are now clear.
I need Jesus every hour,
To heed His blest commands, as I follow Him this day.
Not some mystic place or guru do I need,
But Jesus as the King of Kings upon my heart I seek.

My Jesus is the Star and He beckons me to come
To places where He treads, and I must become
A growing light like Him, so all the world will see
The Light of Jesus flowing, in and out through me.

***

Who Am I ???

I asked the Lord, who am I?
'A blood bought child of God', was His reply.
I asked again, who am I?
His answer echoed through my brain,
'I died so you could live again'.
But who am I? I keep on asking Him.
'A child of Mine, a child of the King of Kings'.

Am I really that important, so special,
To be adopted by the King?
Or am I really muttering, and am I a nothing?
Where did I come from, and,
Where am I going in this wide world of sin?

'You are coming home to Me, in my great Heaven above.
I have bought you with a price and you belong to Me.
I created you with a special purpose in My mind,
To bring you love, and joy, and peace,
And a Heavenly song, to sing all day long.

I created you to bring My light into this world of sin,
And I stand right here with you,
To make sure that you will shine
With all the talents and the gifts – a present from the King
To His own daughter – the daughter of the King.
You are of Royal Blood – which Blood was shed for you
At Calvary's cross, so many years ago.

I chose you with your warts and foibles that are there.
But these, they do not matter, when love is in the air.
I look past these things to see your heart of hearts,
And in the beauty of the moment, I give to you, My love.
And in answer to your question, who am I?
I now give my reply.

You are my precious daughter, the one for whom I died.
And I bequeath to you, the longings of your heart.
Sons and daughters shall return and not again will part,
But shall stay and become one with the heart of God in you.
And you will see this blessing as on your knees you fall
To praise and worship Me, more, and more, and more.'

***

God's Time

It is time, the Lord, He says,
Time for Me to raise the dead,
Time to raise the standard high
Lifting it high up to the sky.

It is time to name the Name of the Lord.
It is time to believe His every Word.
It is time, so it seems, to be filled with Him,
To refute all other claims and salute only Him.

It is time for the Lord to show His Hand
To do the works of old.
But He calls for a man whom He can use
To be the vessel as He should choose.

Choose me, choose me, we all cry aloud.
But He can see if we are proud
And want power, fame and recognition.
No, the Lord's choice is made by heart,
The heart that will bring Him adulation.

But Lord, we prophesy and claim your Name.
Why would you reject our claim
To honour ourselves and make our own name?

'Tis not the season to be jolly,
You need repentance in your heart.
To name yourselves is to depart
From My good precepts in every part.

You see my works and you want the same.
But you don't know My heart or know My Name.
My Name is above reproach
And that is why I come with a different approach.
The pure in heart, the humble in spirit,
I choose these to flow in My Holy Spirit.

***

Testing the Victory

You have passed the test, I say to you,
The test that only you could follow through.
The test is over, and the Light has dawned.
You have overcome and the enemy is warned
"Don't mess with Me, you thief, you liar.
Your place is in hell where you will face fire".

I trusted the Lord, but I found it hard
When all things were black, and I did the hard yards.
The tomb was closed, and I couldn't breathe
Until Jesus came and gave me reprieve.
He made a way and the door it did open.
The Sonlight streamed in, and the darkness was broken.

Now I am standing in the Light, a little bemused
But not in fright, for I am standing in His daylight.
The test was severe, the chains they were strong,
But Jesus stood by me, all the day long.
The power of prayer! The power of praise!
This is my song as I enter new days.

***

But thanks be to God, who gives us the victory through our Lord Jesus Christ.

1 Corinthians 15:57 NKJV

For whatever is born of God overcomes the world. And this is the victory that has overcome the world - our faith.

Who is he who overcomes the world, but he who believes that Jesus is the Son of God.

1 John 5:4-5 NKJV

www.ingramcontent.com/pod-product-compliance
Lightning Source LLC
La Vergne TN
LVHW011213080426
835508LV00007B/759